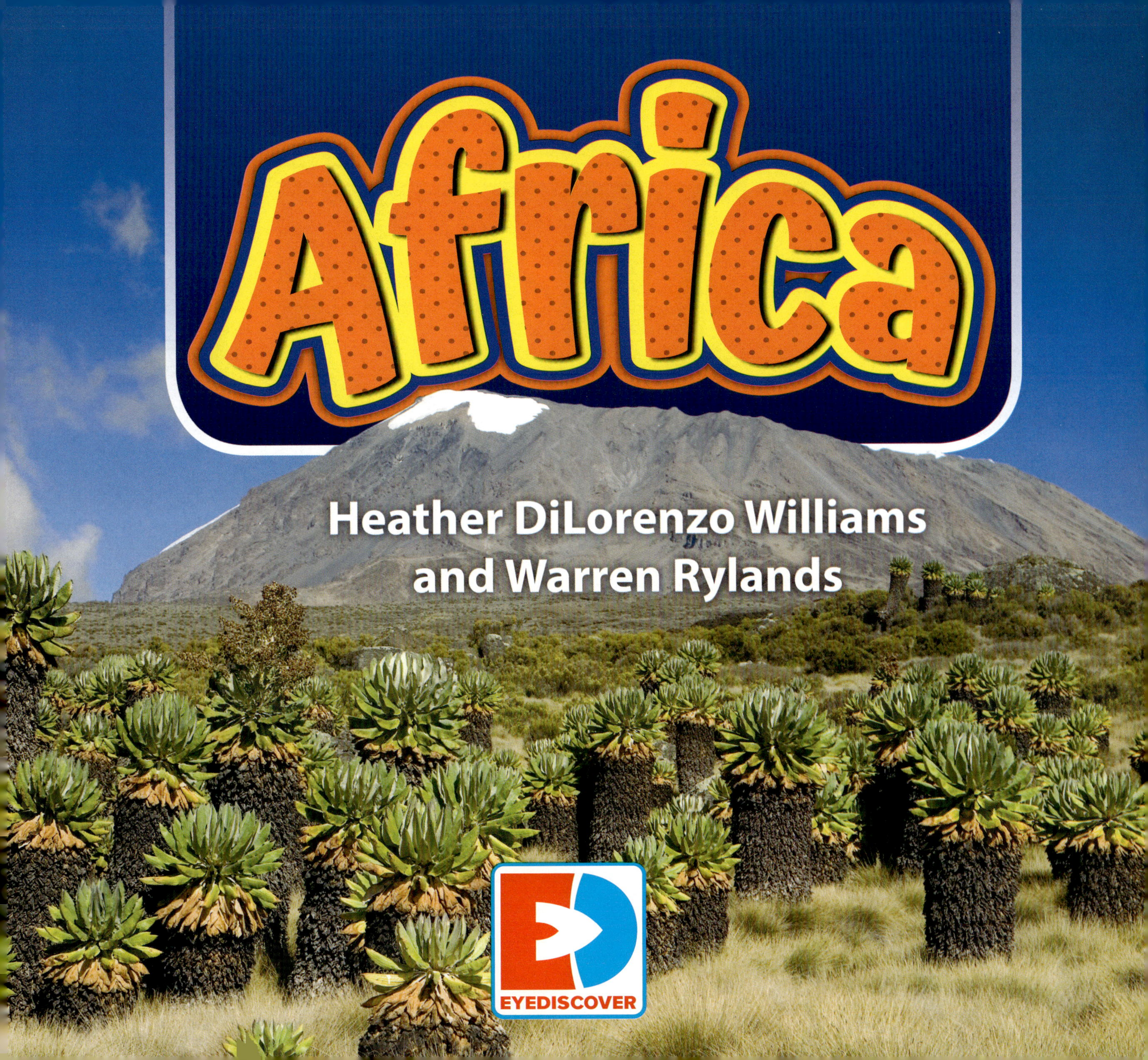
Africa
Heather DiLorenzo Williams
and Warren Rylands
EYEDISCOVER

Go to **www.eyediscover.com** and enter this book's unique code.

BOOK CODE

AVX33337

EYEDISCOVER brings you optic readalongs that support active learning.

Published by AV² by Weigl
350 5th Avenue, 59th Floor New York, NY 10118
Website: www.eyediscover.com

Library of Congress Control Number: 2018953507

ISBN 978-1-4896-8321-2 (hardcover)

Printed in the United States of America
in Brainerd, Minnesota
1 2 3 4 5 6 7 8 9 0 22 21 20 19 18

082018
120917

Project Coordinator: John Willis
Designer: Mandy Christiansen

Weigl acknowledges Alamy, Shutterstock, and iStock as the primary image suppliers for this title.

EYEDISCOVER provides enriched content, optimized for tablet use, that supplements and complements this book. EYEDISCOVER books strive to create inspired learning and engage young minds in a total learning experience.

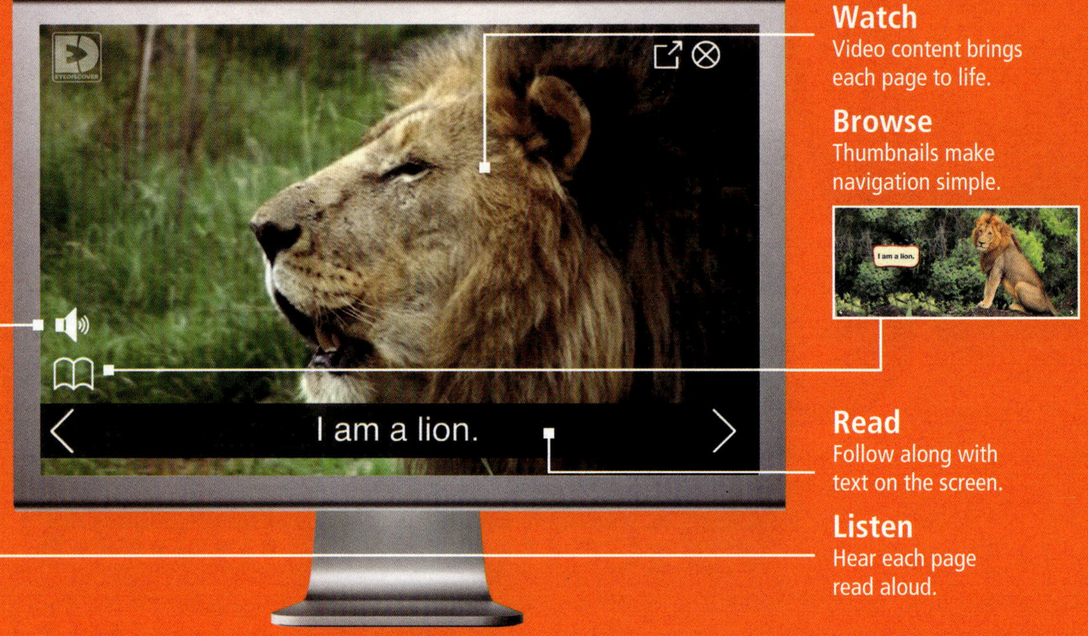

Watch
Video content brings each page to life.

Browse
Thumbnails make navigation simple.

Read
Follow along with text on the screen.

Listen
Hear each page read aloud.

Your EYEDISCOVER Optic Readalongs come alive with...

Audio
Listen to the entire book read aloud.

Video
High resolution videos turn each spread into an optic readalong.

OPTIMIZED FOR

- TABLETS
- WHITEBOARDS
- COMPUTERS
- AND MUCH MORE!

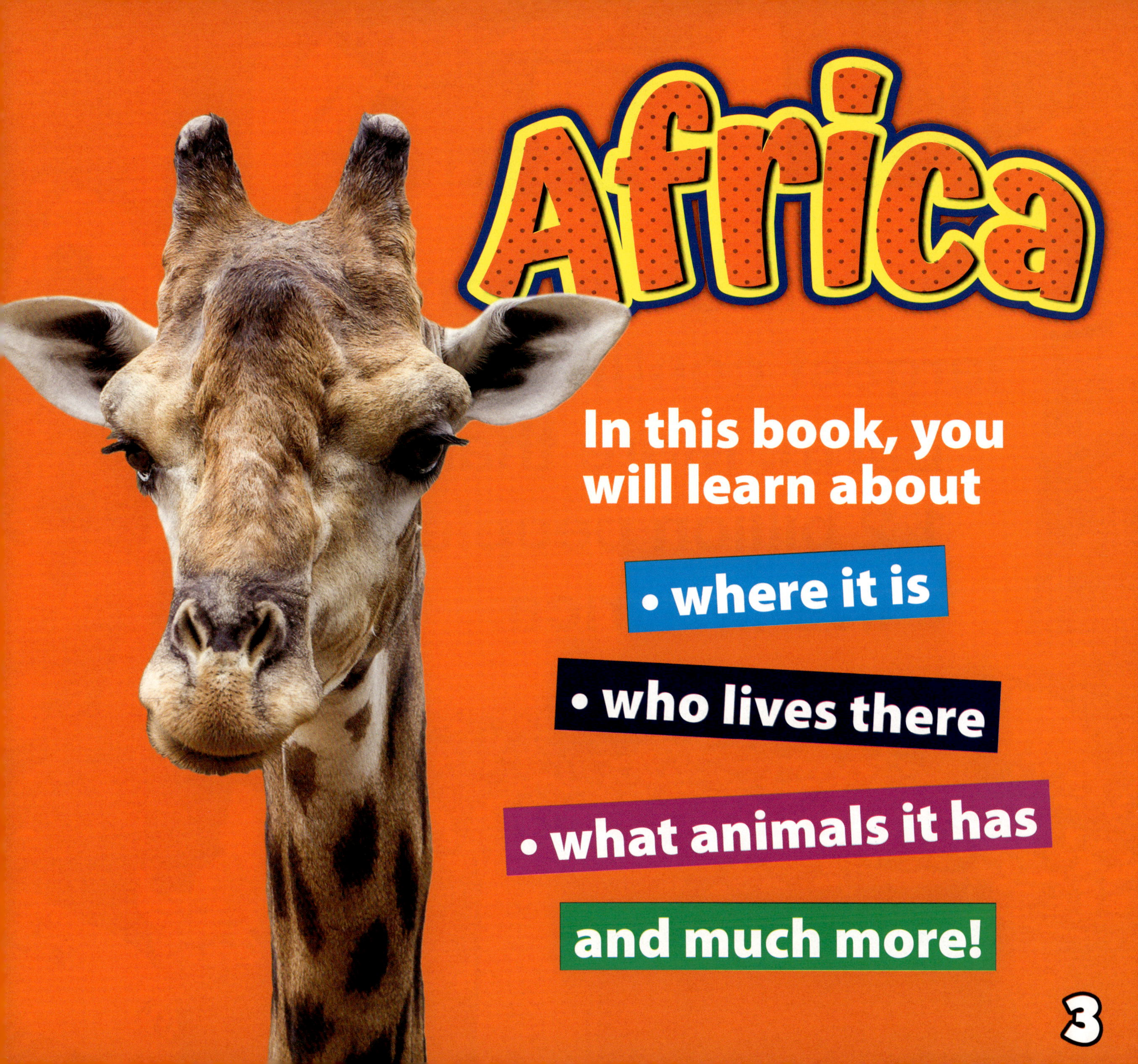

Africa

In this book, you will learn about

- where it is
- who lives there
- what animals it has

and much more!

Africa is the second largest continent on Earth. More than 1.2 billion people live in Africa.

Wakala

6

Lagos, Nigeria, is the biggest African city. About 21 million people live there.

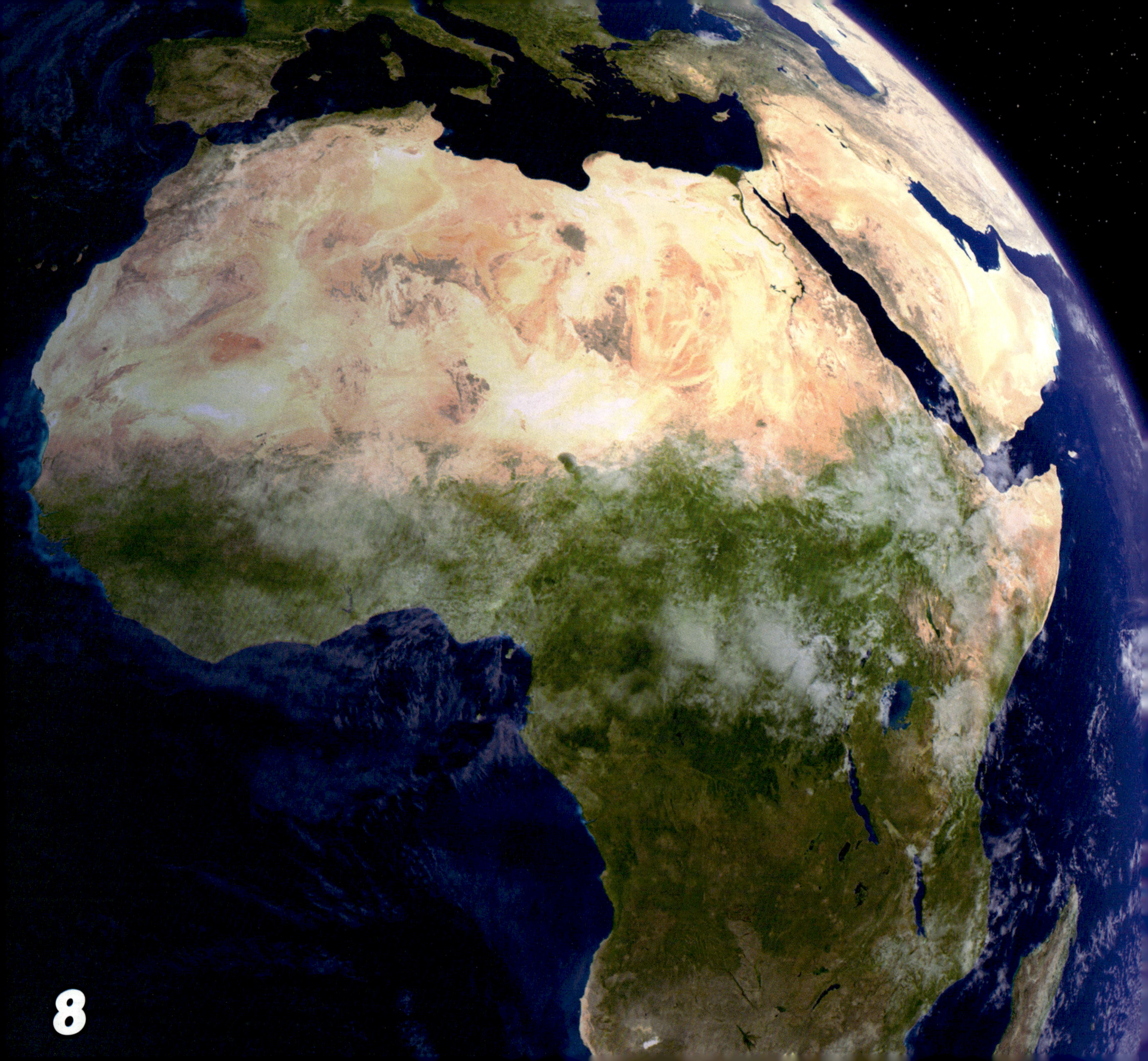

There are 54 countries in Africa. More than 1,500 languages are spoken there.

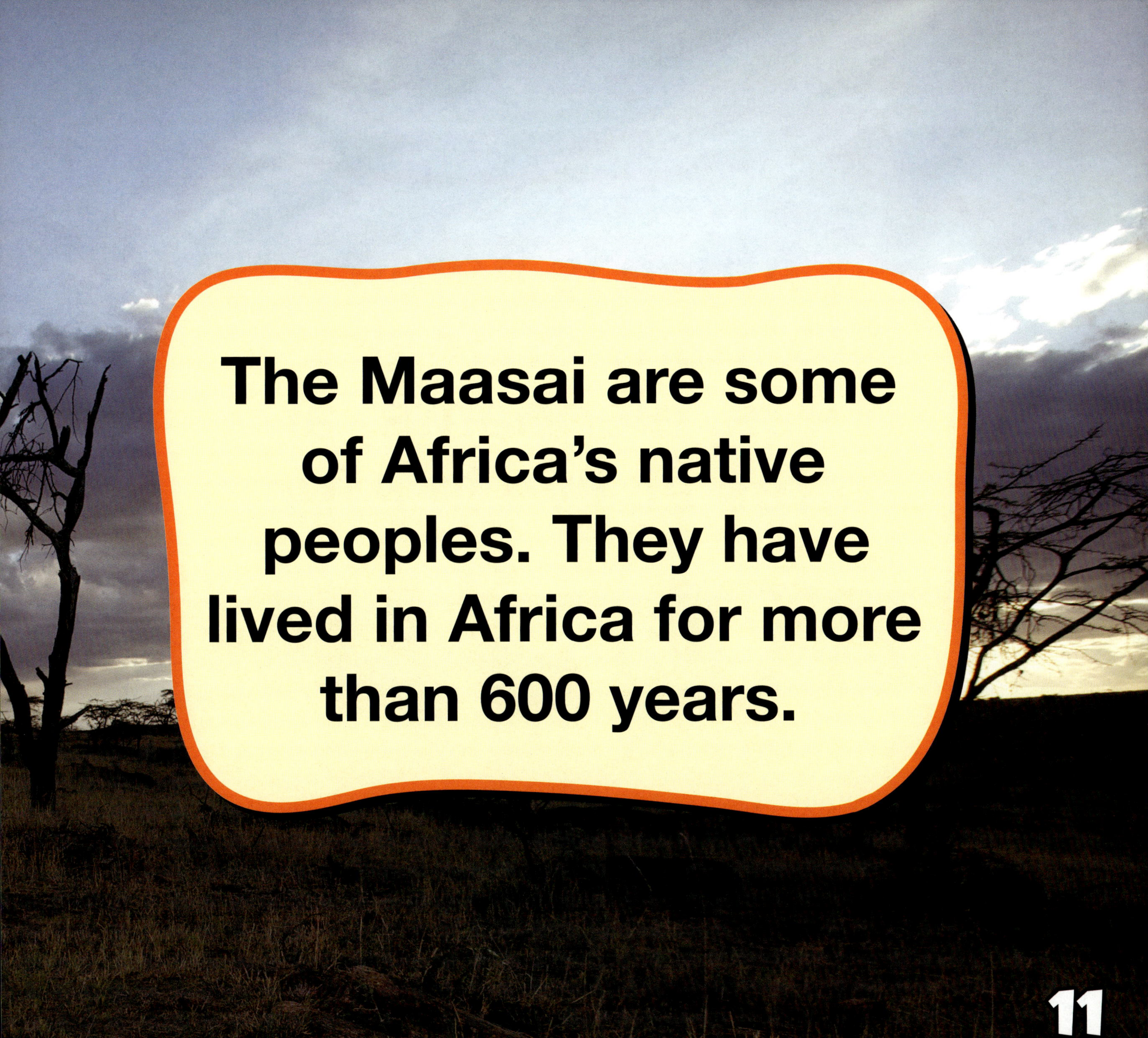

The Maasai are some of Africa's native peoples. They have lived in Africa for more than 600 years.

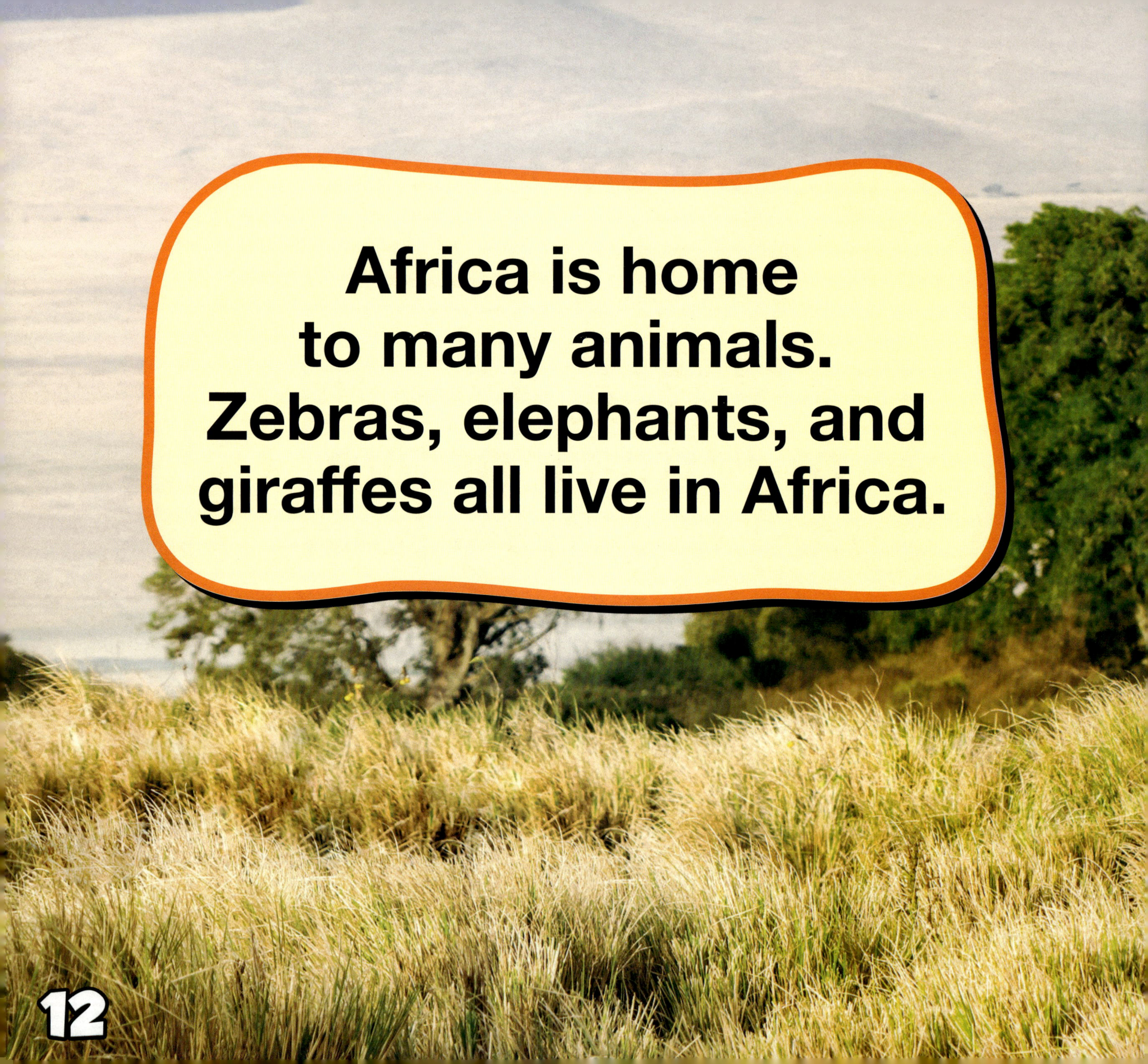

Africa is home to many animals. Zebras, elephants, and giraffes all live in Africa.

Africa is also known for many natural wonders. Victoria Falls is the largest waterfall in the world.

Africa has many mountains. Kilimanjaro is the tallest mountain in Africa.

Africa's Sahara Desert is the largest hot desert in the world.

Many tourists go to Africa every year. It is a beautiful continent to live in and visit.

The Congo rainforest covers about **1.4 million** square miles.

(3.7 million square kilometers)

Africa's smallest country is **Seychelles.** It only covers **177 square miles.**

(459 sq km)

15% of the people in Africa live in the country of **Nigeria.**

Africa's **Nile River** is the longest river in the world. It is **4,258 miles** long. (6,852 km)

About **25,000** people try to climb **Mount Kilimanjaro** each year.

The African island of **Madagascar** is the **fourth-largest** island in the world.

KEY WORDS

Research has shown that as much as 65 percent of all written material published in English is made up of 300 words. These 300 words cannot be taught using pictures or learned by sounding them out. They must be recognized by sight. This book contains 34 common sight words to help young readers improve their reading fluency and comprehension. This book also teaches young readers several important content words, such as proper nouns. These words are paired with pictures to aid in learning and improve understanding.

Page	Sight Words First Appearance
4	Earth, in, is, live, more, on, people, second, than, the
7	about, city, there
9	are
11	for, have, of, some, they, years
12	all, and, animals, home, many, to
15	also, world
16	has, mountains
20	a, every, go, it

Page	Content Words First Appearance
4	Africa, continent, Earth
7	Lagos, Nigeria
9	countries, languages
11	Maasai, native
12	elephants, giraffes, zebras
15	Victoria Falls, waterfall
19	Sahara Desert
20	tourists

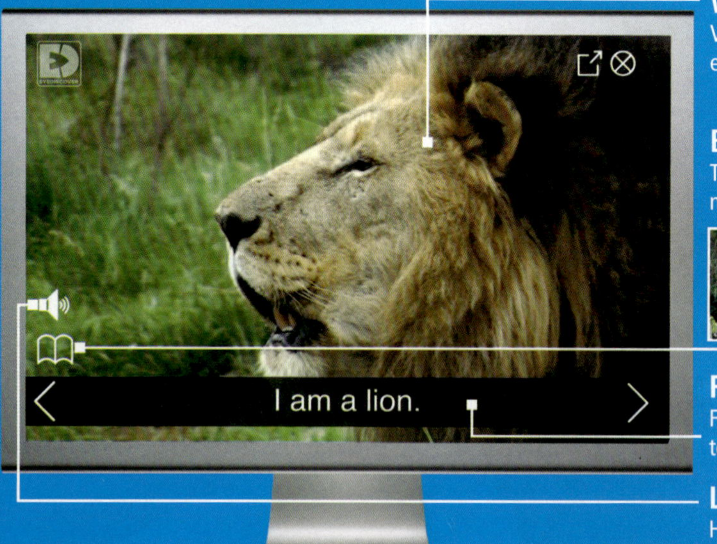

Watch
Video content brings each page to life.

Browse
Thumbnails make navigation simple.

Read
Follow along with text on the screen.

Listen
Hear each page read aloud.

Go to www.eyediscover.com and enter this book's unique code.

BOOK CODE

AVX33337